My HAPPY BOOK

D1743470

Honor Head

ARCTURUS

Sarah Ward

This book has been developed in consultation with Clare Arnold, an art psychotherapist with over 30 years of experience of working with child and adolescent mental health issues.

ARCTURUS

This edition published in 2024 by Arcturus Publishing Limited
26/27 Bickels Yard, 151–153 Bermondsey Street,
London SE1 3HA

Author: Honor Head
Illustrator: Sarah Ward
Consultant: Clare Arnold
Editor: Violet Peto
Designer: Amy McSimpson
Managing Editor: Joe Harris
Design Manager: Rosie Bellwood-Moyler

ISBN: 978-1-3988-4693-7
CH011795NT
Supplier 13, Date 0524, PI 00007608

Printed in China

This is Puppy with his family.

Puppy has lots of different feelings.

This book is about what happens when Puppy feels **happy.**

When you feel
happy, you might
feel like *jumping* ...

... or *skipping* ...

... or *twirling* around.

You might feel like **smiling** and **clapping** and **laughing** until you roll on the floor.

Having fun things to do can make you feel happy. Puppy likes ...

... making a **cake** ...

... drawing a **picture** for someone he loves ...

... and going for a **walk** on a sunny day.

What makes you feel happy?

Spending time with **family** can make you happy.

And playing with your **friends** can, too.

Doing things for other people can make you happy.

Puppy sometimes **gives** his old toys and books to a charity.

He likes to **make** special gifts for his friends, such as bracelets and bookmarks.

What could you make for a friend?

Sharing can make you happy,
and it makes the person you share with happy!

You can share your time
with someone who is alone.

You can make other people happy by being kind.

Even **small things**—like saying something nice—can make someone smile.

Puppy makes his parents happy by helping with chores.

No one is happy all the time.

There will be times when you feel **sad** or **lonely** or **angry.**

If you are feeling unhappy, talk to someone about how you feel.

Draw pictures of what makes you happy. Put them on the wall, or look at them when you feel sad.

Try smiling, even when you don't feel like it.

Smiling can make you feel better.

And when you smile, others smile.

When you are happy, the **whole world** feels very special.

Even being in the rain is fun!

Being happy is a lovely feeling. It makes you feel **safe** and *positive*.

And a **happy hug** is the best kind of hug in the world.

Notes for parents and carers

When children feel safe and happy, they are more likely to have self-confidence, to be willing to try new things, and to follow rules.

- Read through this book with your child, and talk about the things that make you happy. Discuss what makes them happy and unhappy.

- Model a positive outlook for your child. When they are experiencing a challenging situation, try to help them see the upsides.

- Set clear guidelines for your child. Children feel more secure when following a routine.

- Teach your child to be kind, polite, and helpful to everyone, in the home and outside. Explain that other people will respond positively to a cheery, can-do attitude.

- Play and be creative. Let your child's imagination run riot. This can be making dinosaurs or trains with a few cardboard boxes and some crayons. Play and creativity encourage a sense of achievement and happiness.

- Get outside and exercise together. Research has shown that being outside and moving promotes physical and mental health for the whole family.

- Help your child understand that happiness is not the same as being successful or the best at something. Happiness comes through enjoying what you do and trying your best.

- Don't put pressure on your child to pretend to be happy when they feel down. No one feels happy all the time. Reassure your child that you will always be there for them when they feel lonely or sad.